Unpolished

Tracy O'Shea

BookLeaf
Publishing

India | USA | UK

Presentation by *BookLeaf Publishing*

Web: www.bookleafpub.com

E-mail: info@bookleafpub.com

ISBN: 9789358316797

First edition 2023

Daniel

ACKNOWLEDGEMENT

Thank you to my friends, family and colleague's that have cheered me on my journey.
Special thanks to Masha Bennett and the Tribe who are my constant fans. You know who you are.

IBS

Hubble Bubble toil and trouble, That's what
Shakespeare said.
Just guess what's happening to me. I'm not
talking of a pee.

Hubble Bubble toilet trouble, I've got IBS.
If I don't find a loo, I'm gonna make a mess.
I've got so many intolerances; It really makes
me mad.
If I eat the wrong thing my tummy feels so bad
My belly gets distended, it bloats out oh! So
wild,
It gets so very round it looks like I am with
child.

Hubble Bubble toilet trouble, I've got IBS.
If I get offered bread, I never can say yes.
I can't have buns or French stick, a doughnut or
just toast.
I must stick to meat and veg, so I CAN have a
roast!!

I made a mistake the other day, I had Chilli with
chickpeas,

It tasted great to start with, then it brought me to my knees.
A gurgle and a rumble started wrestling in my tum.
I ran as fast as Usain Bolt, to the loo to rest my bum.

Hubble Bubble toilet trouble, I've got IBS.
If I invest in tenner lady, I won't have so much distress.
I've had this awful affliction for over twenty years.
I find it inconvenient; it brings me out in tears.

When I see other people eating vol-au-vents and cake,
I politely decline and smile, but I tell you it's a fake!!

Hubble Bubble toilet trouble, I've got IBS.
Invite me out to dinner, I will always say "OH Yes"!
I love my grub, I love to eat with my family and my friends,
So come on mates, I dare you!
And That's where my story ends…..

Giblets

I've been under the weather. A little bit.
 In fact, I've been feeling. Really shit.
So I decided. To go get some comfort food.
Hoping to lift and raise my mood.

So off I pop. To the shop. I did not stop. Or drop
or flop
And bought, said Comfort Food for my mood.
Chicken and potatoes. My go to when I'm low.
I stumbled home. Not far to go.
My cheeks aglow. I walk very slow.

I plop the chicken in the tin.
Legs spread wide, no longer tied.
And muse at the gaping hole before me.
Where once a bag of giblets would be.

I wonder. Why have all the Giblets gone?
A long time ago. I had a tasty gravy.
Now I rely on granules to save me.
Why have all the giblets gone? Far, far away.

As I pile in the stuffing. By the way, it's mighty
chuffing.
 It's quite my speciality and I'm not bluffing.

I ponder, is there a giblet hoarder? You fucker!!
someone has decluttered My clucker.

 Is the Bisto Empire, a Giblet vampire.
 Someone's earned enough money. Making
granules to retire
Who's made a packet from this giblet racket?
Let's take to the streets in our winter jackets.

Campaign to Parliament to bring giblets back.
Where they belong. In a chicken in a little sack.
We'll go right to the top Protest to Richie Sunak.
Let's see if he's full of giblets or has he got a
bone in his back.

Walk With Me

5

Walk with me on this untrodden path
Wade together through the aftermath
United orphans in our middle age
Our autumn sunset years, another stage.

Come, walk with me
As our sorrow cascades in tears speak
We've been so close, so many years
Shrouded in silence, no need to speak
No words, just allowing our eyes to gently leak.

Walk with me, for just a little while
Accepting the sadness, then learn to smile
Enveloped in grief as it ebbs and flows
Memories drift in on the breeze as it blows
Reminding aching hearts of the past.

Walk with me, as I walk with you
This untrodden path, together my friends
Our footprints make no mark or sound
Soul sisters till we too are in the ground.

Lone Pine Cone

The lone pinecone, Hanging in the tree.
Was it hanging or clinging?
Was it too strong to fall, too attached to let go?
Like all its Siblings.
Why did it need to stay?
It was nestled in between, the bright, lush new
growth.
Surrounded by SAP rising tines, tethered to the
branch.
Like an extra limb or digit, familiar in its stance
Unwavering in the breeze.
Unaffected by the filtered sun, flickering
through the dense branches.
What is so special about this cone?
Sitting high on its regal throne.
How many seasons have come and gone?
Battered and weathered, this dear only one.
Is it still living, growing, or now grown?
Has it hung on to its seeds or are they sown?
What mighty trees a forest Indeed, could grow
from this mighty Cones seeds?
Is it staying till last like the ship's skipper?
Waiting for the others, to flee to safety.
Mothers, fathers, grandparents, and nippers
I saw no sign of mutilated or fallen ones.

Maybe the forest creatures tidy up after supper,
 After chewing and nibling a hearty cone meal,
More likely human intervention.
Or children collected them for a creative
creation.
Still, the lone pinecone holds its own. Strong,
sturdy, knowing its place.
Up so high, not in your face.
Hang in there upon your throne, I'll tell
everyone, I'll get you known,
Stay true. Just be yourself.
Nature 's wonder.
The lone pinecone.

Land of Smelly Breath

Once Upon a Time in the Land of Smelly
Breath. Lived a wrinkly, crinkly old man who
was always close to death.
No one knew his age. He'd been in the village
forever.
Some say he was the founder. I believe this has
his skin looked just like leather.
His hair sprung out of his head in matted Tufts
and clumps.
This just proved he wasn't dead. As he hosted
fleas, nits and ticks.
He was his very own eco-system
Co-existing with nature…and a part time job at
the mortuary.
No one quite knew what he did, but he was
knicknamed "nail it down Sid"
Probably something to do with the coffin lids.
Some say the village was named after him, no
one dare get close enough,
To dare to take a sniff or a whiff , As his breath
maybe the kiss of death.
Luckily his right leg was dead, you can hear him
dragging it from miles ahead,
The landlord loved him, at the local pub,

A couple of rounds and he'd swept the ground,
as his gammy leg was pulled around,
Every one knew when he was bar bound, as they
recognised the itchy scratch sound.
The headless chicken was the local pub. The
centre of the village, quite the social hub.
Two sisters known as the gruesome twosome,
frequented said pub, they were not very
handsome.
Nelly with her smelly belly and her side kick
sister Snotty Lotty with her grotty botty,
It was rumoured, some say, that Nellys smelly
belly was due to an unfortunate fungi infection,
Which was Seconded by her also unfortunate
oozing Pusey boil, an added facial affliction
Nestled neatly on her chinny chin chin,
surrounded by clusters of sprouting hair, both
thick and some thin.
Her sister Snotty Lotty had a permanent slimy
green runny nose, That often dripped onto her
clothes,
 she never smelt her grotty botty, She was
oblivious, it was quite gross.
Nelly however had a crush on Sid, and found out
through the sewer line
That Sid had his good eye on another, Sid had
just the one good eye,
 In the other a rogue nail did fly It was a tragic
incident, you can't deny,

Nelly ranted and raged for days on end, then
decided to confront her lost lover.

The following night, Sid nailed it early. He got
finished by half past eight
Sid shuffled off home to get ready. He didn't
want to be a minute too late.
He dragged himself to the headless chicken. Got
a pint and sat a while.
 Hoping to get a glimpse of Cyclops Sally.
Named so, due to her large emerald, green shiny
eye, nestled quaintly above her nose and an
oozing sty.
 With her long golden mane that shone in the sun
. Run all down her back. No hair on, on her
head. Just down her back.
Sid perched up the corner, so he could watch the
door
Waiting for the lady, he did so adore,
Just then the door flew open, the floor did
vibrate
Then, in stomps, Nelly. She looked very Irate.
She'd been on the homebrew. You always knew.
As She wore only one shoe.
She stumbled and wobbled in a drunken sway.
Looked around, then spotted, Sid across the way.
She shouted and bellowed. OY you!!!,
 Whilst wielding a stick thing in his direction.

"I've got a bone to pick with you".
 Sid recognised the stick she wielded was in fact
a real bone. In his experience from a leg.
 A femur bone!
With a Pointy tip sharpened to perfection, the
ball joint polished and held in her grubby mit.
 Aimed straight at Sid
He stood up aghast on his one good leg,
As she lunged toward him, his mouth opened
wide.
 He breathed out a cloud of bright neon green
haze, as the bone pierced his chest in it did slide
.All At once a huge explosion took place. A
bang and a pop That lit up the place
 Incredibly loud with A puff of smoke and a
mushroom cloud.
This was poor Smelly Nellys mistake by far
As the pointy tip pierced the battery of Sids'
pacemaker
All that was left was two piles of dust
Its true!! That they both did spontaneously
combust.
The landlord rolled his eyes in disgust and
muttered something under his breath
"Dust if I must!"

All in a day in the land of smelly breath
As per norm there had been a death.
For the local folk, they all remain the same

If you're thinking of visiting, please refrain
Many a man woman and child, have been driven insane
By the evil stench like rotten eggs, in the bottom of a drain
You may on occasion, hear a little laughter,
But trust me….very few lived happily ever after.

Invisible

I'm over 60. I'm invisible.
Although I wear bright colours.
I'm quite indistinguishable.
I stand at the bar, awaiting my turn.
The young beauty next to me, will always get
served first.
Doesn't bother them, that I'm dying of thirst.

It comes in quite handy when I've got a touch of
wind.
When the pop, pop, pop from my bottom won't
stop.
I just hold my head high and walk on by.
If I'm invisible? You can't see me? So hopefully
you won't hear or smell me!!
Go IBS. Don't grumble in distress.
Pop off farty pants, as the wind swings your
dress.

I guess it's allowed to blow off now I'm old.
To burp too loud when in a crowd.
That quirky sound can be quite profound.
So burp and fart with all your heart.
If you're over 60, it's OK, you're invisible..

Brain Drain

How do I declutter my head
And fill it with fluffy stuff instead
Can I sweep away the negative thoughts
Put them in a bin of sorts?

How do I declutter my mind
Can I dust away the self-talk I find
Do I beat myself up, like I'd beat a rug
To clear out debris- left over words that still
chug.

So many words spinning in my brain
The endless chatter and clatter is a drain
Please take away this curse in a hearse
The chide inside, these words in herds
That fill my grey matter with endless, useless
pieces of natter.

Put in its place some peace and tranquil
Keep the calmness and just be still.
Breath in freshness like a spring morning
Get rid, declutter the dreadful dark stalker,
That follows me round like a day walker.

Its easier to throw away my pens

Than to declutter my mind, give room to heal,
clear and cleanse,
To give my brain a good spring clean,
So once again my imagination, has room to
glisten and glean.

Silence

When I fall silent
You need to listen
Take in the loudness
Of my heartbeat

Feel the vibration
In the air
When I fall silent
You better beware

My silence is my armour
I do not fight with noise
My body stands alone
In a sturdy meaningful poise

Don't mess with me
When I put my words on hold
I won't waste my breath
Just to look bold

I will hold my own
As the warrior woman I am
You've heard of Boudicca
She and I clasp hands

Silence is my friend
In moments of mistrust
When someone's dirty words
Disintegrate into dust

When I choose silence
I choose not to communicate with you
Take that as a nod
recognise – we're through

Do not utter a single word
Do not use up my O2, my oxygen
This is my space. You turd
Just leave, so I can breathe

Silence once again surrounds me
Shrouds, caresses and is me
Silence my friend, my blanket, my aura
My silence is my armour, I am a warrior.

Belonging

Being a part whilst being apart.
A sense of belonging. Togetherness.
A community of peers.
To wipe up tears. To listen, to hear The fears
To feel alive. Begin to thrive.
Seeds to sow. room to Grow.
The mission. Is discussion.
The beating of hearts. The percussion.
The hunters, the gatherers, bring food to the
table.
To nourish the minds of those less able.
The feeling of being. A longing of belonging.
A unit of unity.
A hub of positivity.
Freedom of speech.
Equal space for each.
Come say your piece.
No, you are heard.
Feel the inner peace.
In every spoken word.

Bench

Sit with me. On this leafy bench.
Amidst the forest full of wonder.
This seat is carved with love and care.
Under the trees of the purest air.

Sit with me on this wooden creation.
Tell me of the seeds you have planted, In your
garden.
In your mind. Your child. In the earth itself.
In this beautiful gift you have, Of inner self.

Sit with me just for a while.
Tell me of the wonders of yourself.
How did it feel? The morn of your first born.
Who knew that love can fill the earth? Your
heart, to overflow.

Sit with me. On this leafy bench.
 Let go of the past. It's had its chance.
 We have this moment
 Let's plant new seeds in rhyme or verse.
 Your imagination as is infinite, As the universe.

Cinderella and her Two Ugly Blisters

She threw down her duster, with all the strength
she could muster,
"I'm don't with this skivvying, I want to start
Living"
She chucked the broom across the room
And set off on her journey.
She wandered through the grassy meadow,
 admiring the mass of wild flowers,
 the arrival of colour, against her skin of pallor
Made her all the more excited,
She was full up with valour.

As she trekked, up hill and down dell, Across
rivers and streams,
She was living the dream, so it did seam,
As night drew near, she needed to rest,
 so found a mossy spot,
She sat down, and truly felt blessed.

It was then that the pain , from her feet came
upon her,
She shook off her shoes, and wiggled her toes,
and rubbed her poor weary soles,

Gently and kindly she reflected on her feat, just
then she noticed two lumps on her feet.

She turned her feet up to look underneath, and to
her absolute horror,
Two enormous blisters stared right back at her.
As she touched the hot swollen lumps, she cried
out "oh! what a bother".
"Oh no, I now have two ugly blisters, to replace
my 2 very ugly sisters!"

As she spoke the words, the blisters took shape,
her mouth full open, agape.
The blisters started to form a face, where was
she? What is this place?
Glaring back at her, were 2 little faces, gnarly
and angry, little gazes.
Oy, Cinderella, what have you done?
You've walked us to death,
now you've got the cheek to stop and take a
breath,
The next time you choose to run away, get some
proper shoes with a cushion underlay.
 Now that you have a callous or two, what on
earth are you going to do?

Cinders was stunned, no words would come out,
She stuttered and stammered a muffled response,

" oh, I do apologize, I just wanted a life, now
I've got you two
Are you husband and wife?"
You're welcome to come along on my
adventurous journey,
Only you both are just a little burnie,
I know what I'll do, before I return you to my
shoe,
I'll cover you both with some soft fluffy moss,
It will keep you warm and extra comfy,
And in the morning if you are able,
We'll all live together, like Cane and Abel.

Green

Green is the colour of nature.
Surrounded by all shades. Is my nurture.
All around my soul. Enveloped in green.
New awakening life. Yet to be seen.
Alas. The buds up on the tree.
Remind me, There's more green in Me
For in others, I have come to trust.
And now the truth, Has turned this to dust.
My voice echoes in the shadows.
I stand up for my peers, My dear fellows.
Ignite the fire, with my bellows,
Stand together like the mighty oak tree
As Whilst there's a drop of green blood in me.
I won't rollover or bow down.
I'll stand tall, and straighten my crown.

Homeless Guy

People rush by, the homeless guy,
Slumped over, leaning against a cold concrete
pillar,
Busy workers, pass by on their lunch hour,
Where the well-off walk, the long way round.

He doesn't notice – sat with his bags,
And an empty costa cup – hoping.
To hear the chink of small change,
Will he eat today, or again go hungry.

Is this his chosen lifestyle?
Or a victim of circumstance?
What was his life before this?
He's someone's son or brother,
I wonder…where's his mother?

Ukulele

I love my ukulele, I play it day and night
I play it in the morning and then again at night,
I might play it at lunchtime, then again, might
not…

A strange thing occurred the other day,
Whilst I prepared to play,
That ukulele came alive, got up and ran away…

Its little legs were running, as fast as it could go,
I shouted "oye Ukie, come back,
 I need you in my life".
It looked at me straight in the eye and this is
what it said….

"you crazy ukulele lady, you can't even play,
You bash me and abuse me, almost night and
day,
I'm getting out of here right now,
Before you get the chance, to sing and dance and
prance,
You think you are so great when you grab me in
that stance!!

You sing along, you're out of tune,

The beats all wrong, I've had enough,
Unless you show improvement, I'm never
coming back.

I've put up with all your yodelling
Ha! It's just out of tune yelling,
You're bonkers and you know it,
You crazy ukulele woman
I've packed my bag, I'm outta here….
Before you do more damage, and now I need a
therapist,
To heal my strings from carnage.

You bash me and you beat me, you strum away
with pride,
I just wish you'd bugger off and leave me alone
to bide".

I stood aghast at what I'd heard, I really was
quite shaken,
I'd given all I had to give; I'm trying to learn a
rhythm.
That ungrateful ukulele, is "mine" it's a given,
I bought it on the marketplace, all comfy in case,
So, I decided to respond, the only way I know
how….

"Hey Uke, my love, please don't leave,
I didn't mean to hurt you; I promise to try harder

To strum a little more in tune, I get so much
enjoyment.
Please try to understand me, I'm really not a
loon"

"Can we sit down and just talk a bit, And see
what we can work out,
I'll try to sing along in tune, not be so loud and
shout,
I may be a crazy uke woman, that's true as the
day is long,
You breathed a breath of life in me, that's
overdue and welcome,
I promise I will learn, to play a little ditty,
Come on little Uke, on this crazy woman,
 please take some pity."

Wheelbarrow

The wheelbarrow stood alone in the shadows
Amidst the autumn leaves.
No-one to push him around anymore.
No-one putting leaves in the barrow...
The wheelbarrow looked sad and lonely,
Moonlight drifted across, accentuating his
emptiness,
His barrow was empty, no longer half full,
The front wheel let out a little air…PFFFTs
And rested on his rear legs.
The barrow was left in the lane
Not far from home.
Why was he here all alone,
Do I have no use anymore?
Have I just become a barrow bore?
His paint flaked a little at the thought,
Of the day his owner first saw him and bought
him.
This bright shiny barrow,
All new young and agile,
Able to carry a heavy load,
 How hard he used to work, No load did he ever
shirk,
Eager to have his bucket filled, with cut down
bushes and twigs.

A cart for children to run up and down, He
always smiled, never a frown.
Now they're grown, the nest they have flown.
The wheelbarrow let out another great big sigh
 PFFFTs
Alas the front wheel flattened a little more
Will I ever be of use again?
Am I headed for the bin?
The night fell heavy upon the cold metal bucket
Damp and dewy during the night.
As the dawn broke the barrow was at his
lowest…
Alas, in the distance he saw a light, heard a
slight crunch in the night
As it came closer, he saw a bicycle light
It stopped in front of his flattened wheel
They had a look round, muttering was heard
Wheelbarrow tried to stand proud
They tapped his sides, checked his tyre, picked
up his handles,
Pushed him to and fro
Muttered more words, then had to go.
He sank further into the muddy ground
Surrounded by colourful leaves all around,
Yet listen. A familiar sound
The trees whispered in the wind,
The gentle breeze swirled in the trees,
Autumn leaves fluttered down, and one by one
They lifted his frown,

During the day his bucket started to fill
Many leaves a plethora of colour came and
rested
Until his bucket was full, heaped, overflowing
Oh joy! I'm useful, my confidence growing
So proud he puffed up and stood proud,
His tyre magickly full and firm,
Shiny paint glistened in the afternoon sun.
Someone passed having a run
Then, a noise from the distance, came ever
closer,
The bicycle from this morning was returning.
Suddenly, out of nowhere, a cat jumped forward
And nestled in the leaves
The cat snuggled down to have a rest, purring
gently in their nest
The voice from the bicycle calmly said
"oh there you are my silly kitty, you had me
worried, full of pity,
Come on home to get warm and eat, by the fire
on your warm seat"
The cat just purred, they wouldn't budge, even
when the person gave them a kindly nudge.
"oh well, there's just one thing to do" ….

Wrinkly

When are you officially a wrinkly?
We know the age of a baby, a tween and a teen,
Middle age is a bit ambiguous,
What age that is, I'm at a loss

Were the laughter lines, the very first signs?
Have the years of belly laughs and smiles
Left shelves of skin, like orderly files,
Lines and lines, of concertinaed skin,
Did I laugh too much, just on a whim.

When did the cute brown freckles, evolve into
age spots,
From tiny little dots, to great big spots, you can
now join up the dots,
On top of that, I'm at risk of clots,
 When did my collagen, get up and run,
Did I look the other way whist having fun,
Or maybe forgot my factor 50, when out in the
sun,
I really don't remember, my memory evades
me!!
Like the day I saw fowl jowls, in the mirror
staring back at me!!

I don't have the answers, so I put it in a verse,
Hoping to get results from the universe,
One thing I know from years of experience,
Don't cough to hard, or sneeze too often,
As you will get both wrinkles and accidental
tinkles.

The Key

She pushed the key into the ancient key hole,
She had no idea what she might find,
Granny had lost it, misplaced this key,
Many moons ago, feels like a century.

Just like magic the old lock clicked open,
She waited tentatively, it felt wrong to disturb.
Will she find something that may perturb?
Slowly, carefully she slid the open the drawer,

Oh! what's this silky fabric,
As she held it up high
It's old granny's bloomers. Her great big
drawers,
And look here! Theres some writing, on the
backside.

She took it over to the light,
And got a bit of a fright,
She flattened out the silky knickers.
And tried to decipher. By a light that weirdly
flickers.

This is what she read…

To my dearest naughty myrtle
You simply are the best,
Now its time for me to rest,
I'm off to war tomorrow.
Much love always
Horny Harold. XX

AH! She gasped, throwing down the pants in
disgust,
Naughty Myrtle, my kind little grandma,
Had shenanigans -not with my grandpa,
Horny Harold! Who the heck are you?
Ill never know, as nanna left us, far too soon.
Do I tell, do I not? I'm put on the spot!

With a great big slam, she shut the drawer
As her uncle walked in the door,
Hello Uncle Harold! Hhhh how are you?...

Tribute

They called themselves the 3 musketeers,
Though quite often found themselves in tears,
Huddled around a half empty bottle of wine,
Having a whinge and whine,
Ching ching of glasses
As they recall loves losses.

In fact thew were more like Shakespeare's 3
witches,
Hubble bubble, lots of trouble, more their motto,
little bitches!
At school, inseparable, then working in a
factory, deplorable,
Then, as life and love took course, its toll
No longer time these days to Rock and Roll.

As I stand here flowers and bananas in hand
Remembering the shenanigans we spread across
the land,
We didn't see life as fragile
Until it was… shattered,
Like a spade to the head,
Banged up to date with the latest tech,
Not iPad, iPhone or zoom tech,
But neuro surgeons and life support machines,

I start to shake with shock, standing outside my
comrades room,
Masked up, gloved up, keep my germs to
myself!

Scared

To see what has become, of one of my dearest
oldest friends.
Clot, embolism, "inoperable tumour"
Sounds to heavy a weight to contemplate.
I peer through the blinds of the mechanical
container,
Bleep bleep…bleep bleep…

Wires running everywhere like spaghetti…
I gasp, my throat closes, I can't breathe,
My heart stops working for a moment,
As I see the hairless skin covered skeleton
That once was, still is, I'm confused…

My dancing, prancing buddy,
Such a natural mover, such gloriousness
She was wonderous to watch,
She tried to be our teacher,
I couldn't even manage the macarena!
She overflowed with life, love enthusiasm and
motivation,
The mischief maker, the hip shaker,

Street dancing, magical, moving, motions.
Like a movie in front of us, she just loved to
move.

We were in awe; she never made a thing of it…
My mind moves back to the memory,
When we went to a Summer Solstice Gathering,
She was barefoot for 3 days, face painted like a
fairy,
Just moving, grooving, dancing round the
midnight fire circle,
Like a golden firefly, spinning and flitting.
As the dry wood spat and hissed
As more fuel was piled on.

I forgot myself momentarily,
Smiled outwardly, almost laughed to myself,
As the memories of our youth and boundless
energy
Seep back into my veins.

Gretel (an alternative Fairy Tale)

Dearest Quasi my love,
I am so grateful that you rescued me
From the clutches of the nasty witch,
In a cage she did me shove,
All those moons ago.

And Notre Dame is no shabby show.
Far more decent than a wooden cabin
That my gambling dad won on a lottery win
However my love,
 Now I must leave,
For I know you have wonky eyes,
That strayed,
No longer just for me…

I saw you with my good eye
Chatting up that there Heidi
I see you no longer love me.

As I grab my coat,
I realise you only want her for her goat,
Something I can never give you,
Even though I stink like goat poo
And what people say about me is not wrong,

I do smell strong; I really do pong.

You see Quasi me dearest,
I learnt a thing or three
From the evil dastardly witch,
When I was hiding in a ditch
I did spy
With my good eye,
She collected a mushroom
That send people to their doom.

I collected said shroom same,
I share with you and your shame.

So as you sip your tea
I will quietly flee,
Just remember …
You can't hide your lying eye
Beneath cap, gown, or mono brow frown,
And as I tie my pretty bonnet,
And whisper to myself a sonnet,

So long as men can breathe or eyes can see,
So long lives this and gives life to thee
….only for a minute or three….he he…

(ref Shakespeare sonnet 18, last 2 lines)

The Garden in my Brain

The Garden in my Brain, Needs a bit of
weeding,
It's had lots of scratches and splinters, and had
its share of internal bleeding,
Theres a corner over there, that's dark and just a
bit dingy,
Its where I swear and do lots of whinging,
Theres glowing bits, full of sparkle, that shine
beyond the dark
It shimmers over the "many a debacle" when I
wish to mute the dog, to NO bark,
When my head feels like it might explode, or
implode, or just …plode

The plants that grow in my garden, I cultivated
from seed,
No degree or PHD, engineered by me, I'm an
experimentee,
It often feels like a jungle, as I battle my way
through.
Not sure what I'm looking for, although I often
find the answer,
At the end of my pen.

Like a spade it does some digging, prunes away
like secateurs,
Pulling out the weeds, that I no longer need,
Repurposing to the compost heap, maybe next
year, a better yield I'll reap.
As I navigate my autumn years, addressing the
distressing,
No longer hiding from my tears, let the sun
shine,
In the Garden in my Brain
And rejoice, even when there's a little rain.

Unpolished

Untethered, unleashed, escaped.
Wild woman poet on the loose
Do not disturb, she may become perturbed!
Letting go… of anger and rage,
Tears and fears spill out on the page.
As her pen slips into top gear,
21 poems in 21 days
From her journal, doesn't lift her gaze.
Emptying her head, perched on the bed,
As she scribes rows and rows
Her pen flows and flows with prose.
Arthritic fingers hold the pen tight,
Not losing focus, the light is in sight.
Where will this adventure take her, no one
knows,
The twists and turns of life, as she grows.
Dot the I's and cross the t's,
Many have said, unpolished is she.

Its gone past midnight, time to sleep,
Until the morning and the 7 o'clock bleep.
Rest now little one, its time to just be,
She hasn't escaped, she's been set free.

www.ingramcontent.com/pod-product-compliance
Lightning Source LLC
LaVergne TN
LVHW021308200726
843509LV00012B/1842